It's Easy To Play Chopin.

EXCLUSIVELY DISTRIBUTED BY

HAL•LEONARD®

This book © Copyright 1988 by
Wise Publications
UK ISBN 0.7119.1522.9
Order No. AM 71747

Art direction by Mike Bell
Cover illustration by Paul Leith
Compiled by Peter Evans
Arranged by Christopher Norton

Berceuse

Composed by Frederik Chopin

Etude No.3

Composed by Frederik Chopin

Funeral March From Sonata
Opus 35 No.2

Composed by Frederik Chopin

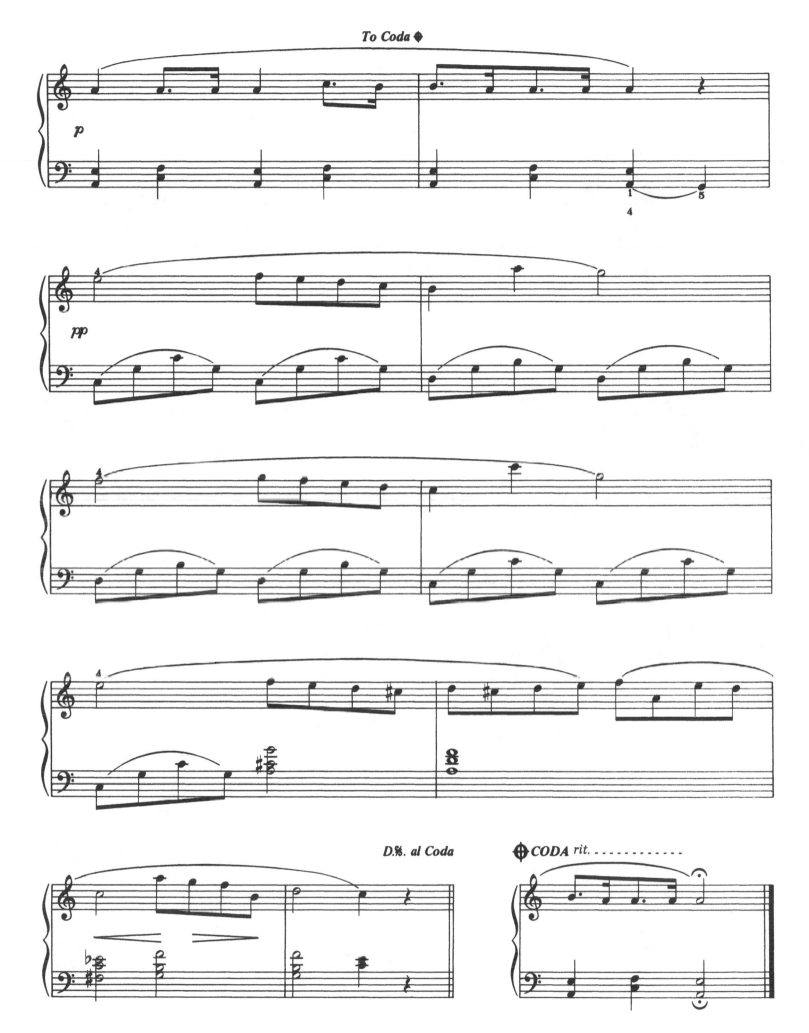

Mazurka Opus 7 No.1

Composed by Frederik Chopin

Mazurka Opus 33 No.2

Composed by Frederik Chopin

Allegro moderato

Nocturne Opus 9 No.2

Composed by Frederik Chopin

Prelude Opus 28 No.7

Composed by Frederik Chopin

Nocturne Opus 15 No.3

Composed by Frederik Chopin

Polonaise Opus 40 No.1

Composed by Frederik Chopin

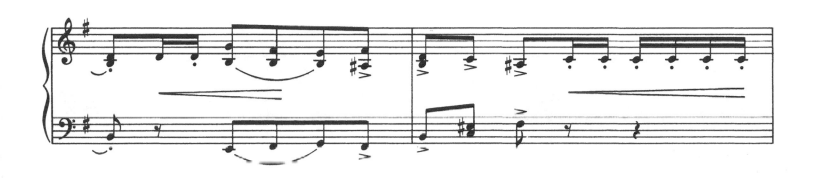

D.C. al Fine

poco rit.

21

Prelude Opus 28 No.4

Composed by Frederik Chopin

Nocturne Opus 55 No.1

Composed by Frederik Chopin

D.%. al Coda

rit. -

CODA

26

Waltz Opus 18

Composed by Frederik Chopin

Nocturne Opus 72 No.1

Composed by Frederik Chopin

poco a poco cresc. . . . .

f

dim.

p

p

29

Waltz Opus 34 No.1

Composed by Frederik Chopin

Polonaise Opus 53

Composed by Frederik Chopin

Prelude (Raindrop)
Opus 28 No.15

Composed by Frederik Chopin

Waltz Opus 64 No.2

Composed by Frederik Chopin

Theme From Sonata Opus 58

Composed by Frederik Chopin

Prelude Opus 28 No.20

Composed by Frederik Chopin

Theme From Ballade Opus 23

Composed by Frederik Chopin

Waltz Opus 69 No.1

Composed by Frederik Chopin

Theme From Fantaisic Impromptu
Opus 66

Composed by Frederik Chopin

Waltz Opus 69 No.2

Composed by Frederik Chopin

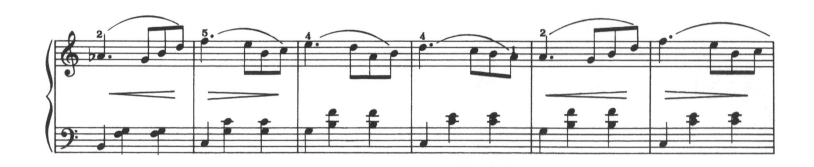

2/06(57864)

Bringing you the words and the music

All the latest music in print... rock & pop plus jazz, blues, country, classical and the best in West End show scores.

- Books to match your favourite CDs.

- Book-and-CD titles with high quality backing tracks for you to play along to. Now you can play guitar or piano with your favourite artist... or simply sing along!

- Audition songbooks with CD backing tracks for both male and female singers for all those with stars in their eyes.

- Can't read music? No problem, you can still play all the hits with our wide range of chord songbooks.

- Check out our range of instrumental tutorial titles, taking you from novice to expert in no time at all!

- Musical show scores include *The Phantom Of The Opera*, *Les Misérables*, *Mamma Mia* and many more hit productions.

- DVD master classes featuring the techniques of top artists.